FAVORITE BRAND NAME™

Low-Sugar
BAKING COOKBOOK

Publications International, Ltd.
Favorite Brand Name Recipes at www.fbnr.com

Pictured on the front cover: Rich Chocolate Cheesecake *(page 32)*.

Pictured on the back cover *(from top to bottom):* Cranberry Sunshine Muffins *(page 68)*, Reduced-Sugar Chocolate Chip Cookies *(page 38)* and Nectarine-Blueberry Crisp *(page 8)*.

ISBN: 1-4127-2403-1

Manufactured in China.

8 7 6 5 4 3 2 1

Nutritional Analysis: The nutritional information that appears with each recipe was submitted in part by the participating companies and associations. Every effort has been made to check the accuracy of these numbers. However, because numerous variables account for a wide range of values for certain foods, nutritive analyses in this book should be considered approximate.

Microwave Cooking: Microwave ovens vary in wattage. Use the cooking times as guidelines and check for doneness before adding more time.

Preparation/Cooking Times: Preparation times are based on the approximate amount of time required to assemble the recipe before cooking, baking, chilling or serving. These times include preparation steps such as measuring, chopping and mixing. The fact that some preparations and cooking can be done simultaneously is taken into account. Preparation of optional ingredients and serving suggestions is not included.

Table of Contents

Low-Sugar Baking

Americans love sweets—cookies, cakes, pies, doughnuts, sweet rolls and candy, to name just a few. The problem? These sweet foods are laden with sugar and other sweeteners. They tend to be high in calories and low in essential nutrients. Plus, they are often high in fat, particularly the "bad" kinds of fat—saturated fat and trans fat. There's no question that American's love for sweets has been a contributing factor to our country's current weight problems.

If you are trying to reduce sugar in your diet, this cookbook is for you. Whether you want to lose weight, have been diagnosed with diabetes, or just wish to eat more nutritiously, you'll find *Low-Sugar Baking Cookbook* a useful addition to your library.

Baking with sugar substitutes is one of the most popular ways to reduce sugar in your diet. For those who can't use sugar substitutes, there are recipes in this publication that rely on small amounts of sugar or a combination of sugar and sugar substitutes. Since sugar has several functions in baked goods other than providing sweetness, recipes that incorporate some sugar often give good results.

Sugar is one of the ingredients (fat is another) that make cakes, cookies, muffins and breads tender and give them their characteristic texture. Cookies rely on sugar for spreading during baking. Sugar also helps give baked goods their golden brown exterior color. Baked goods made with sugar stay fresh longer. In addition, brown sugar and molasses contribute more flavor, a darker color and more moistness to baked goods than granulated sugar does.

Low-Sugar and Sugar-Free Techniques for Baking

SUGAR SUBSTITUTES

- Aspartame- and sucralose-based substitutes can easily replace sugar in fillings, cheesecakes, sweet sauces and glazes.

- For best results use cookie, cake, muffin and quick bread recipes specially developed for sugar substitutes.

- Replace up to 50 percent of the sugar in your favorite cake, cookie, muffin or quick bread recipe with a sugar substitute that measures like sugar. Finished products may differ slightly in tenderness, texture, color and keeping qualities from those of the sugar-based recipe.

- If you wish to replace all of the sugar with sugar substitutes, refer to the manufacturers' Web sites for more guidance.

- New products that blend either sucralose or aspartame with sugar are now available. Use them to replace the sugar in your favorite recipes. Refer to the manufacturers' instructions for guidance.

Sugar

- Reduce the amount of sugar in a cake, cookie, muffin or quick bread recipe by one fourth or one third. You may be surprised to find you like the less sweet result.

- Replace one third to one half of the sugar in baked goods with fruit such as applesauce, mashed bananas or dried fruit.

- Substitute fruit spreads for jellies and preserves in baked goods. Fruit spreads, which can be found with jellies in the supermarket, are made without added sugar.

- Moist cakes often don't need to be frosted. Instead, lightly sprinkle them with powdered sugar.

- Instead of frosting cookies or cakes, try melting bittersweet chocolate with a little cream or fat-free half-and-half for a quick, low-sugar glaze.

Delectable Desserts

Nectarine-Blueberry Crisp

3 cups cubed unpeeled
    nectarines

2 cups fresh blueberries

2 tablespoons granulated
    sugar

1 tablespoon cornstarch

½ teaspoon ground
    cinnamon

¼ cup all-purpose flour

¼ cup uncooked quick oats

¼ cup chopped walnuts

3 tablespoons packed dark
    brown sugar

2 tablespoons toasted
    wheat germ

2 tablespoons reduced-fat
    margarine, melted

¼ teaspoon ground nutmeg

1 Preheat oven to 400°F. Spray bottom and side of 9-inch round or square baking pan with nonstick cooking spray. Combine nectarines, blueberries, granulated sugar, cornstarch and cinnamon in medium bowl. Transfer to prepared pan; bake 15 minutes.

2 Meanwhile, combine remaining ingredients in small bowl, stirring with fork until crumbly. Remove fruit mixture from oven; sprinkle with topping. Bake 20 minutes longer or until fruit is bubbly and topping is lightly browned. Serve warm. *Makes 6 servings*

Calories: 211 (23% of calories from fat), Total Fat: 6g, Saturated Fat: <1g, Carbohydrate: 38g, Cholesterol: 0mg, Protein: 4g, Sodium: 51mg, Dietary Fiber: 4g

Exchanges: 1 Starch, 1½ Fruit, 1 Fat

Prep Time: 13 minutes

4 cups frozen sliced peaches, thawed and juices reserved

¼ cup packed dark brown sugar

1 tablespoon cornstarch

1 to 2 tablespoons water

1 tablespoon lemon juice (optional)

1 teaspoon vanilla

¼ teaspoon almond extract

½ cup uncooked quick oats

2 tablespoons all-purpose flour

2 tablespoons sugar substitute*

½ to ¾ teaspoon ground cinnamon

⅛ teaspoon salt

¼ cup (½ stick) cold reduced-fat butter, cut into small pieces

Fat-free whipped topping (optional)

1 Preheat oven to 375°F. Spray 9-inch pie plate with nonstick cooking spray; set aside.

2 Combine peaches with juices, brown sugar, cornstarch, water, lemon juice, if desired, vanilla and almond extract in medium bowl. Toss until cornstarch is dissolved. Transfer to prepared pie plate.

3 Combine oats, flour, sugar substitute, cinnamon and salt in medium bowl. Cut in butter with pastry blender or two knives until mixture resembles coarse crumbs. Sprinkle over peaches.

4 Bake 25 minutes or until bubbly at edges. Cool 20 minutes on wire rack. Top each serving with dollop of whipped topping, if desired. *Makes 8 (½-cup) servings*

This recipe was tested with sucralose-based sugar substitute.

Calories: 146 (35% of calories from fat), Total Fat: 6g, Saturated Fat: 4g, Carbohydrate: 24g, Cholesterol: 15mg, Protein: 2g, Sodium: 41mg, Dietary Fiber: 2g

Exchanges: 1 Starch, ½ Fruit, 1 Fat

Prep time: 20 minutes
Bake time: 50 to 60 minutes
Chill time: 1½ hours

CRUST

- ¾ **cup ice water**
- 1 **teaspoon vinegar (white or cider)**
- 2 **cups all-purpose flour, divided**
- 3 **tablespoons SPLENDA® Granular**
- 7 **tablespoons vegetable shortening**

FILLING

- 7 **cups Granny Smith apples, peeled, cored, sliced**
- ⅔ **cup SPLENDA® Granular**
- 3 **tablespoons cornstarch**
- ¾ **teaspoon cinnamon**
- ⅛ **teaspoon salt**

MIX ice water and vinegar in a cup. Place ½ cup flour in bowl, adding vinegar-water mix gradually; whisk well. Combine remaining flour and SPLENDA® Granular in medium bowl. Add shortening, using pastry cutter or two knives to cut in until mixture is crumbly. Gradually add water-flour mixture, adding just enough to bind dough together.

DIVIDE dough in half. Gently pat each half into circle on a floured work surface. Cover circles separately with plastic wrap; chill 30 minutes.

PREHEAT oven to 375°F. Spray 9-inch pie pan with nonstick cooking spray. Set aside.

TOSS filling ingredients together in a large mixing bowl.

ROLL out dough on a lightly floured work surface into a circle 11 inches in diameter. Place in prepared pie pan and add filling. Roll out remaining dough and cover filling. Crimp edges together with fingertips or fork. Use fork to prick top crust. Brush crust with milk, if desired, for more golden, even browning.

BAKE 50 to 60 minutes or until crust is golden. Cool pie at least 1 hour before serving.

Makes 1 (9-inch) pie (8 slices)

Calories: 289 (35% of calories from fat), Total Fat: 11g, Saturated Fat: 3g, Carbohydrate: 44g, Cholesterol: 0mg, Protein: 3g, Sodium: 39mg, Dietary Fiber: 4g

Exchanges: 1 Starch, 2 Fruit, 2 Fat

1 Preheat oven to 350°F. Lightly spray 2-quart baking dish. Combine breads, apples and raisins in prepared dish. Whisk half-and-half, egg substitute, sugar substitute, butter flavoring, vanilla, cinnamon, nutmeg and salt in large bowl until blended. Pour over bread mixture.

2 Let mixture stand 15 minutes; stir every 5 minutes to coat bread evenly. Bake 45 to 50 minutes or until set. Serve warm.   *Makes 8 servings*

SERVING SUGGESTION: Drizzle each dessert plate with 1 teaspoon sugar-free caramel sauce and top with a warm square of bread pudding.

Calories: 120 (5% of calories from fat), Total Fat: 1g, Saturated Fat: 0g, Carbohydrate: 23g, Cholesterol: 7mg, Protein: 5g, Sodium: 251mg, Dietary Fiber: 2g

Exchanges: 1 Starch, ½ Fruit, ½ Lean Meat

2 cups French bread cubes

2 cups multigrain bread cubes

2 cups chopped unpeeled apples

⅓ cup golden raisins

1½ cups nonfat half-and-half

¾ cup cholesterol-free egg substitute

½ cup sugar substitute

2 tablespoons liquid butter flavoring

1 teaspoon vanilla

1 teaspoon ground cinnamon

½ teaspoon ground nutmeg

¼ teaspoon salt

Prep Time: 20 minutes

Bake Time: 30 minutes

1¼ **cups all-purpose flour**

½ **cup plus 2 tablespoons sugar substitute,* divided**

2 **tablespoons granulated sugar**

1¼ **teaspoons baking powder**

¼ **teaspoon baking soda**

¼ **teaspoon salt**

⅔ **cup low-fat buttermilk**

¼ **cup plus 2 tablespoons cholesterol-free egg substitute, divided**

2 **tablespoons butter, melted**

1 **teaspoon vanilla**

2 **ounces reduced-fat cream cheese, softened**

1¼ **cups fresh or frozen raspberries, thawed**

1 **tablespoon powdered sugar**

1 Preheat oven to 375°F. Lightly coat 9-inch round baking pan with nonstick cooking spray; set aside.

2 Combine flour, ½ cup sugar substitute, granulated sugar, baking powder, baking soda and salt in large bowl. Combine buttermilk, ¼ cup egg substitute, butter and vanilla in small bowl; add to flour mixture. Stir until blended. Spread in prepared pan.

3 Beat cream cheese and remaining 2 tablespoons sugar substitute in small bowl with electric mixer at medium speed until blended. Beat in remaining 2 tablespoons egg substitute.

4 Sprinkle raspberries over batter. Drop spoonfuls of cheese mixture over top. Bake 30 to 33 minutes or until toothpick inserted into center comes out clean. Cool 10 minutes on wire rack. Sprinkle with powdered sugar. Serve warm. *Makes 8 servings*

*This recipe was tested with sucralose-based sugar substitute.

Calories: 185 (21% of calories from fat), Total Fat: 5g, Saturated Fat: 3g, Carbohydrate: 38g, Cholesterol: 13mg, Protein: 5g, Sodium: 241mg, Dietary Fiber: 2g

Exchanges: 2 Starch, ½ Fruit, ½ Lean Meat, ½ Fat

1½ cups all-purpose flour

¼ teaspoon salt

⅓ cup canola oil

1 teaspoon almond extract

3 to 4 tablespoons ice
    water

3 pears

¼ cup SPLENDA® No
    Calorie Sweetener,
    Granular

2 tablespoons no-sugar
    apricot preserves,
    melted

1 tablespoon dried
    cranberries

1 tablespoon slivered
    almonds (optional)

1 Preheat oven to 350°F. Lightly coat baking sheet with
nonstick cooking spray.

2 In medium bowl, mix together flour and salt. While
stirring flour mixture briskly with fork, drizzle in oil a little
at a time, stirring until mixture resembles coarse crumbs.
Add almond extract and water a tablespoon at a time,
adding just enough water for dough to come together.
Shape dough into disk. Wrap in waxed paper or plastic
wrap; refrigerate 1 hour or until firm.

3 While dough chills, peel pears and slice in half lengthwise.
Core pears by cutting a "V"-shaped wedge lengthwise
from the center of the cut side of each pear. Place halves
in bowl of water mixed with a little lemon juice.

4 On baking sheet, roll out dough into rectangle. Drain
pears and slice thinly. Insert knife blade under slices and
lift onto dough. Repeat with remaining slices. Fold dough
edges over to form border. Sprinkle pears with
SPLENDA®. Brush pears and dough with preserves.
Sprinkle pears with cranberries and almonds, if using.

5 Bake 30 minutes or until top is golden brown. Cool on
wire rack. Slice into squares to serve.   *Makes 10 servings*

*Calories: 167 (41% of calories from fat), Total Fat: 8g, Saturated Fat: <1g,
Carbohydrate: 23g, Cholesterol: 0mg, Protein: 2g, Sodium: 60mg,
Dietary Fiber: 2g*

Exchanges: 1 Starch, 1 Fruit, 1 Fat

Prep Time: 10 minutes
Bake Time: 20 minutes

2 cups pear slices

2 cups frozen peach slices, partially thawed

2 tablespoons raisins

1/4 cup water

4 packets sugar substitute, divided

2 teaspoons cornstarch

1/4 teaspoon vanilla or vanilla, butter and nut flavoring

1 cup reduced-fat baking mix

1/2 cup plain nonfat yogurt

2 tablespoons reduced-fat margarine, melted

1 teaspoon grated orange peel

1/4 teaspoon ground cinnamon

1 Preheat oven to 425°F.

2 Spray 11×7-inch baking dish with nonstick cooking spray. Add pears, peaches and raisins; set aside.

3 Combine water, 3 packets sugar substitute, cornstarch and vanilla in medium bowl; stir until cornstarch dissolves. Pour over fruit mixture in baking dish; toss gently to blend.

4 Combine baking mix, yogurt, margarine, remaining 1 packet sugar substitute, orange peel and cinnamon in medium bowl; stir until well blended. Mixture will resemble stiff batter. Spoon batter onto pear mixture in 8 mounds. Bake 20 minutes or until crust is light brown. Serve warm or at room temperature.

Makes 8 (1/2-cup) servings

Calories: 144 (16% of calories from fat), Total Fat: 3g, Saturated Fat: <1g, Carbohydrate: 29g, Cholesterol: <1mg, Protein: 3g, Sodium: 235mg, Dietary Fiber: 3g

Exchanges: 1 Starch, 1 Fruit, 1/2 Fat

Preheat oven to 425°F. Spray a baking sheet with butter-flavored cooking spray. Place 2 cups strawberries in a large bowl. Mash well with fork or potato masher. Stir in ½ cup SPLENDA® Granular. Add remaining 4 cups strawberries.

Mix well to combine baking mix and remaining ¼ cup SPLENDA® Granular. Add milk and sour cream. Mix well until a soft dough forms. Drop batter by spoonfuls onto prepared baking sheet to form 6 shortcakes. Bake for 7 to 9 minutes or until golden brown. Place baking sheet on a wire rack and let stand for 10 minutes. For each serving, place a shortcake on a dessert dish and spoon about ¾ cup strawberry sauce over top.

Makes 6 servings (1 shortcake plus ¾ cup sauce)

Favorite recipe from *SPLENDA® Recipes developed by JoAnne Lund,* *www.healthyexchanges.com*

Calories: 162 (22% of calories from fat), Total Fat: 4g, Saturated Fat: <1g, Carbohydrate: 29g, Cholesterol: <1mg, Protein: 3g, Sodium: 293mg, Dietary Fiber: 4g

Exchanges: 1 Starch, 1 Fruit

6 cups chopped fresh strawberries

¾ cup SPLENDA® No Calorie Sweetener, Granular, divided

1 cup plus 2 tablespoons reduced-fat biscuit baking mix

⅓ cup fat-free milk

2 tablespoons no-fat sour cream

1 jar (10 ounces) maraschino cherries, drained, stems removed, halved

1¼ cups graham cracker crumbs

2 tablespoons canola oil

2 packages (8 ounces each) fat-free cream cheese, softened

1 package (8 ounces) reduced-fat cream cheese, softened

1 cup SPLENDA® No Calorie Sweetener, Granular

1 cup cholesterol-free egg substitute

½ cup nonfat evaporated milk

2 teaspoons almond extract

¼ teaspoon salt

1 can (8 ounces) crushed pineapple in its own juice, drained

1 Preheat oven to 325°F. Line mini muffin baking pans with cupcake liners. Place cherry half in bottom of each cup.

2 Place crumbs in medium bowl. While briskly stirring crumbs with fork, drizzle in oil a little at a time, stirring until mixture resembles coarse crumbs.

3 In large bowl, beat cream cheese with mixer at high speed until smooth. Add SPLENDA®, egg substitute, milk, almond extract and salt. Beat until smooth. Chop remaining cherries; stir into filling with pineapple. Spoon filling into each muffin cup, covering cherries. Sprinkle each cup with crust mixture. Press crust lightly into filling.

4 Place pan on baking sheet. Bake 15 to 20 minutes or until filling puffs and begins to crack. Cool on wire rack. Refrigerate 4 to 6 hours or overnight before serving. To serve, peel away cupcake liners and invert gems cherry-side up onto serving plate.

Makes 16 servings (about 48 bite-sized gems)

Calories: 160 (30% of calories from fat), Total Fat: 5g, Saturated Fat: 2g, Carbohydrate: 19g, Cholesterol: 9mg, Protein: 8g, Sodium: 364mg, Dietary Fiber: <1g

Exchanges: ½ Starch, 1 Fruit, ½ Fat, 1 Lean Meat

Best-Loved
Cakes

Java-Spiked Walnut Coffee **Cake**

Prep Time: 30 minutes
Bake Time: 30 minutes

2 tablespoons sugar-free
   fat-free mocha instant
   coffee mix

¼ teaspoon ground
   cinnamon

1½ cups all-purpose flour

¼ cup sugar substitute*

¼ cup granulated sugar

1 teaspoon baking powder

½ teaspoon baking soda

⅛ teaspoon salt

1 container (6 ounces)
   plain fat-free yogurt

¼ cup cholesterol-free egg
   substitute

2 tablespoons butter,
   melted

1 teaspoon vanilla

¼ cup finely chopped
   walnuts

1 Preheat oven to 350°F. Spray 8×8-inch baking pan with nonstick cooking spray; set aside.

2 Combine coffee mix and cinnamon in small bowl; set aside.

3 Combine flour, sugar substitute, granulated sugar, baking powder, baking soda and salt in large bowl. Combine yogurt, egg substitute, butter and vanilla in small bowl; add to flour mixture. Stir just until moistened.

4 Spread batter into prepared pan. Sprinkle with reserved coffee mixture. Sprinkle with walnuts. Bake 30 to 35 minutes or until wooden toothpick inserted into center comes out clean. Serve warm. Cut into 9 pieces.

Makes 9 servings

*This recipe was tested with sucralose-based sugar substitute.

Calories: 166 (28% of calories from fat), Total Fat: 5g, Saturated Fat: 2g, Carbohydrate: 25g, Cholesterol: 8mg, Protein: 4g, Sodium: 212mg, Dietary Fiber: 1g

Exchanges: 2 Starch, 1 Fat

Chocolate Orange Cake **Roll**

Prep Time: 20 minutes

Bake Time: 12 to 15 minutes

⅓ **cup all-purpose flour**

¼ **cup plus 1 tablespoon unsweetened cocoa powder, divided**

¼ **teaspoon baking soda**

4 eggs, separated

½ **teaspoon vanilla**

¼ **cup sugar substitute***

½ **cup plus 2 tablespoons granulated sugar, divided**

½ **cup orange fruit spread**

1 Preheat oven to 375°F. Spray 15×10×1-inch jelly-roll pan with nonstick cooking spray. Dust with flour. Set aside.

2 Combine flour, ¼ cup cocoa and baking soda in small bowl; set aside.

3 Beat 4 egg yolks and vanilla in large bowl with electric mixer at high speed 5 to 6 minutes or until thick and light colored. Gradually add sugar substitute and 2 tablespoons granulated sugar, beating well after each addition.

4 Beat 4 egg whites in another large bowl with electric mixer at high speed until soft peaks form. Gradually add remaining ½ cup granulated sugar; beat until stiff peaks form.

5 Gently fold egg yolk mixture into egg white mixture. Sift flour mixture over egg mixture. Gently fold flour mixture into egg mixture just until blended. Spread evenly into prepared pan. Bake 12 to 15 minutes or until top springs back when lightly touched.

6 Meanwhile, sprinkle remaining 1 tablespoon cocoa onto one side of clean towel. Use narrow spatula to loosen edges of cake from pan. Invert pan onto prepared towel. Roll up towel and cake, starting from short side. Cool on wire rack. Unroll cake. Remove towel. Spread cake with orange spread. Roll up cake. Cut into 10 slices.

Makes 10 servings

This recipe was tested with sucralose-based sugar substitute.

Calories: 136 (15% of calories from fat), Total Fat: 2g, Saturated Fat: 1g, Carbohydrate: 25g, Cholesterol: 85mg, Protein: 3g, Sodium: 60mg, Dietary Fiber: 1g

Exchanges: 1½ Starch, ½ Fat

3 cups all-purpose flour

2 teaspoons ground
cinnamon

1 teaspoon baking soda

1 teaspoon ground nutmeg

1 teaspoon ground cloves

½ teaspoon baking powder

½ teaspoon salt

1 cup sugar substitute

½ cup canola oil

½ cup unsweetened
applesauce

¾ cup egg substitute

1 can (15 ounces) solid
pumpkin (about 2 cups)

1 Preheat oven to 325°F. Spray 13×9-inch baking pan with nonstick cooking spray; set aside. Combine flour, cinnamon, baking soda, nutmeg, cloves, baking powder and salt in medium bowl; set aside.

2 Combine sugar substitute, oil and applesauce in large bowl. Beat 1 minute with electric mixer at medium speed until smooth. Beat in egg substitute and pumpkin until well blended.

3 Gradually add flour mixture to pumpkin mixture, beating until just blended. Do not overmix.

4 Pour batter into prepared pan. Bake 1 hour and 20 minutes or until toothpick inserted in center comes out clean. Cool completely in pan on wire rack. Cut into 24 pieces.   *Makes 24 servings*

Calories: 114 (31% of calories from fat), Total Fat: 4g, Saturated Fat: 0g, Carbohydrate: 14g, Cholesterol: 0mg, Protein: 2g, Sodium: 126mg, Dietary Fiber: 1g

Exchanges: 2 Starch, 1 Fat

Coat a 9-inch springform pan with cooking spray. Sprinkle graham cracker crumbs evenly over the bottom of pan. Set aside. Process the cream cheese, sour cream and ricotta cheese in a food processor until smooth. Add the peanut butter and mix. Slowly add the sugar and vanilla extract. Slowly pour the eggs through the food chute with the processor running. Process until blended. Spoon the mixture over the graham cracker crumbs. Bake in a preheated 300°F oven for 50 minutes. Center will be soft, but will firm when chilled. Turn the oven off and leave the cheesecake in the oven for 30 minutes more. Remove from oven; let cool to room temperature on a wire rack. Cover and chill 8 hours. Serve with assorted fresh berries, if desired.

Makes 10 servings

Favorite recipe from *Peanut Advisory Board*

Calories: 140 (32% of calories from fat), Total Fat: 5g, Saturated Fat: 2g, Carbohydrate: 14g, Cholesterol: 10mg, Protein: 13g, Sodium: 240mg, Dietary Fiber: 0g

Exchanges: 1 Starch, 1 Lean Meat, ½ Fat

½ cup low-fat graham cracker crumbs

8 ounces light cream cheese, cut into cubes

8 ounces fat-free cream cheese, cut into cubes

½ cup fat-free sour cream

½ cup fat-free ricotta or low-fat cottage cheese

⅓ cup peanut butter

½ cup firmly packed dark brown sugar

2 teaspoons vanilla extract

6 egg whites *or* ¾ cup egg substitute

Bittersweet Chocolate Torte

Torte

6 tablespoons stick butter or margarine

4 ounces unsweetened chocolate

⅓ cup fat-free milk

⅓ cup sugar-free apricot preserves or apricot spreadable fruit

2 teaspoons instant coffee crystals

1 egg yolk

1 teaspoon vanilla

1½ cups EQUAL® SPOONFUL*

3 egg whites

⅛ teaspoon cream of tartar

¼ cup all-purpose flour

⅛ teaspoon salt

Rich Chocolate Glaze

1 ounce semi-sweet chocolate

1 tablespoon stick butter or margarine

Whipped topping, fresh raspberries and/or fresh mint (optional)

- For Torte, heat 6 tablespoons butter, 4 ounces unsweetened chocolate, milk, preserves and coffee crystals in small saucepan, whisking frequently until chocolate is almost melted.

- Remove pan from heat; continue whisking until chocolate is melted and mixture is smooth. Whisk in egg yolk and vanilla; add Equal® Spoonful, whisking until smooth.

- Lightly grease bottom of 8-inch cake pan and line with parchment or waxed paper. Beat egg whites and cream of tartar to stiff peaks in large bowl. Fold chocolate mixture into egg whites; fold in combined flour and salt. Pour cake batter into pan.

- Bake in preheated 350°F oven 20 to 25 minutes or until wooden pick inserted in center comes out clean. Do not overbake. Carefully loosen side of cake from pan with small sharp knife, which will keep cake from cracking as it cools. Cool cake completely in pan on wire rack; refrigerate 1 to 2 hours or until chilled.

- For Rich Chocolate Glaze, melt 1 ounce semi-sweet chocolate and 1 tablespoon butter in small saucepan, stirring frequently.

- Remove cake from pan and place on serving plate. Pour Rich Chocolate Glaze over top of cake, letting it run down sides. Let cake stand about 1 hour or until glaze is set. Garnish top of cake with whipped topping, fresh raspberries and fresh mint.

Makes 12 servings

May substitute 36 packets EQUAL® sweetener.

Calories: 145 (68% of calories from fat), Total Fat: 11g, Saturated Fat: 7g, Carbohydrate: 11g, Cholesterol: 18mg, Protein: 3g, Sodium: 110mg, Dietary Fiber: 2g

Exchanges: 1 Starch, 2 Fat

CAKE

1 cup all-purpose flour

⅓ cup granulated sugar

10 packets sugar substitute
_or_ equivalent of
20 teaspoons sugar

3 tablespoons
unsweetened
cocoa powder

2 teaspoons baking powder

½ cup warm fat-free
(skim) milk

2 tablespoons canola oil

2 teaspoons vanilla

½ teaspoon salt

SAUCE

¼ cup granulated sugar

10 packets sugar substitute
_or_ equivalent of
20 teaspoons sugar

3 tablespoons
unsweetened
cocoa powder

1¾ cups boiling water

1 Preheat oven to 350°F. Combine all cake ingredients in large bowl; beat 2 minutes with electric mixer at medium speed until well blended. Pour into ungreased 9-inch square baking pan.

2 To prepare sauce, sprinkle ¼ cup granulated sugar, 10 packets sugar substitute and 3 tablespoons cocoa over batter in pan. Pour boiling water over top. _Do not stir._

3 Bake 40 minutes or until cake portion has risen to top of pan and sauce is bubbly underneath. Cut into 9 squares. Serve immediately. _Makes 9 servings_

Calories: 150 (18% of calories from fat), Total Fat: 3g, Saturated Fat: <1g, Carbohydrate: 26g, Cholesterol: <1mg, Protein: 4g, Sodium: 246mg, Dietary Fiber: <1g

Exchanges: 1½ Starch, ½ Fat

1 Preheat oven to 325°F. Line 15×10-inch jelly-roll pan with waxed paper.

2 Combine flour and sugar substitute in small bowl.

3 Beat egg whites in large bowl with electric mixer at high speed until foamy. Add vanilla and cream of tartar. Beat until soft peaks form. Gradually add granulated sugar, beating until stiff peaks form. Sift ⅓ of flour mixture over egg white mixture. Fold in. Repeat with remaining flour mixture. Spread into prepared pan. Bake 20 minutes or until top springs back when lightly touched.

4 Meanwhile, lightly sprinkle powdered sugar over one side of clean towel. Use narrow spatula to loosen edges of cake from pan. Invert pan over prepared towel. Roll up towel and cake, starting from short side. Cool on wire rack.

5 Unroll cake. Remove towel. Spread with ice cream. Roll up cake. Wrap in plastic wrap. Freeze at least 2 hours or until firm.

6 Cut cake into 10 slices to serve. Top each serving with 1 sliced strawberry.   *Makes 10 servings*

This recipe was tested with sucralose-based sugar substitute.

Calories: 134 (27% of calories from fat), Total Fat: 4g, Saturated Fat: 2g, Carbohydrate: 26g, Cholesterol: 18mg, Protein: 4g, Sodium: 48mg, Dietary Fiber: 2g

Exchanges: 1½ Starch, ½ Lean Meat, ½ Fat

Prep Time: 15 minutes
Bake Time: 20 minutes
Cool Time: ½ hour
Freeze Time: 2 hours

- **½ cup sifted cake flour**
- **¼ cup sugar substitute***
- **6 egg whites**
- **¾ teaspoon vanilla**
- **½ teaspoon cream of tartar**
- **⅓ cup granulated sugar**
- **1 tablespoon powdered sugar**
- **1 pint sugar-free, reduced-fat strawberry ice cream, softened**
- **10 strawberries**

1 cup chocolate wafer crumbs

3 tablespoons EQUAL® SPOONFUL*

3 tablespoons stick butter or margarine, melted

3 packages (8 ounces each) reduced-fat cream cheese, softened

1¼ cups EQUAL® SPOONFUL**

2 eggs

2 egg whites

2 tablespoons cornstarch

¼ teaspoon salt

1 cup reduced-fat sour cream

2 teaspoons vanilla

4 ounces (4 squares) semi-sweet chocolate, melted and slightly cooled

- Mix chocolate crumbs, 3 tablespoons Equal® Spoonful and melted butter in bottom of 9-inch springform pan. Pat mixture evenly onto bottom of pan. Bake in preheated 325°F oven 8 minutes. Cool on wire rack.

- Beat cream cheese and 1¼ cups Equal® Spoonful in large bowl until fluffy; beat in eggs, egg whites, cornstarch and salt. Beat in sour cream and vanilla until well blended. Gently fold in melted chocolate. Pour batter into crust.

- Bake in 325°F oven 40 to 45 minutes or until center is almost set. Remove cheesecake to wire rack. Gently run metal spatula around rim of pan to loosen cake. Let cheesecake cool completely; cover and refrigerate several hours or overnight before serving. To serve, remove side of springform pan. *Makes 16 servings*

May substitute 4½ packets EQUAL® sweetener.

***May substitute 30 packets EQUAL® sweetener.*

Calories: 219 (58% of calories from fat), Total Fat: 14g, Saturated Fat: 9g, Carbohydrate: 15g, Cholesterol: 57mg, Protein: 7g, Sodium: 313mg, Dietary Fiber: 1g

Exchanges: 1 Starch, 3 Fat

1½ cups cake flour

2½ teaspoons baking powder

Pinch salt

1¼ cups sugar substitute*

6 tablespoons buttermilk

¼ cup canola oil

¼ cup lemon juice

2 egg yolks

Grated peel of 1 lemon

1 teaspoon vanilla

6 egg whites, at room
temperature

½ teaspoon cream of tartar

2 tablespoons granulated
sugar

2 teaspoons powdered
sugar (optional)

1 Preheat oven to 325°F. Sift together flour, baking powder and salt in medium bowl. Stir in sugar substitute; set aside.

2 Combine buttermilk, oil, lemon juice, egg yolks, lemon peel and vanilla in large bowl; beat 1 minute at medium speed of electric mixer until smooth. Add flour mixture, beating at low speed until blended. Beat 30 seconds on medium or until smooth.

3 In separate bowl, with clean beaters, beat egg whites and cream of tartar until foamy. Gradually add granulated sugar; beat until egg whites are stiff but not dry.

4 Gently fold ¼ of whites into prepared batter; fold in remainder of whites. Spoon batter into ungreased 10-inch tube pan, spreading evenly.

5 Bake 30 minutes or until cake springs back when gently touched. Cool upside down by placing pan on bottle or funnel for 45 minutes. Sift powdered sugar over cake before serving, if desired.   *Makes 10 servings*

This recipe was tested with sucralose-based sugar substitute.

Calories: 157 (38% of calories from fat), Total Fat: 7g, Saturated Fat: <1g, Carbohydrate: 20g, Cholesterol: 43mg, Protein: 4g, Sodium: 168mg, Dietary Fiber: <1g

Exchanges: 1 Starch, 1½ Fat

1 Preheat oven to 325°F. Slice bananas into ¼-inch slices.

2 Combine ½ cup sugar and water. Heat over medium-high heat, stirring mixture and swirling pan until sugar is amber in color. Remove from heat. Stir in butter. Pour mixture immediately into 8×8-inch round nonstick baking pan. Arrange sliced bananas in caramel on bottom of pan.

3 Sift flour, baking powder and salt; set aside. Beat sugar substitute, oil and applesauce 1 minute in large bowl on medium speed of electric mixer. Beat in egg whites and yolk, one at a time until blended. Beat in buttermilk and vanilla. Gradually add flour mixture, beating until blended.

4 Pour batter over bananas in pan. Bake 30 to 35 minutes or until toothpick inserted in center comes out clean. Cool 5 minutes in pan on wire rack. Invert cake onto plate.

Makes 12 servings

2 small bananas

½ cup sugar

1 tablespoon water

2 tablespoons butter

1½ cups all-purpose flour

2 teaspoons baking powder

½ teaspoon salt

¾ cup sugar substitute*

¼ cup canola oil

¼ cup unsweetened applesauce

3 egg whites

1 egg yolk

½ cup low-fat buttermilk

1 teaspoon vanilla

Calories: 184 (35% of calories from fat), Total Fat: 7g, Saturated Fat: 2g, Carbohydrate: 27g, Cholesterol: 23mg, Protein: 3g, Sodium: 191mg, Dietary Fiber: 1g

Exchanges: 1½ Starch, ½ Fruit, 1 Fat

2 unpeeled Bosc or Anjou pears, cored and thinly sliced

3 tablespoons fresh lemon juice

1 tablespoon melted butter

1 tablespoon packed brown sugar

1 cup all-purpose flour

1 teaspoon baking powder

1 teaspoon ground cinnamon

¼ teaspoon baking soda

⅛ teaspoon salt

⅓ cup fat-free (skim) milk

1 egg

3 tablespoons apricot fruit spread

1 tablespoon vegetable oil

1 tablespoon minced fresh ginger

1 Preheat oven to 375°F. Spray 10-inch deep-dish pie pan with nonstick cooking spray; set aside.

2 Toss pears in lemon juice; drain. Brush butter evenly onto bottom of prepared pan; sprinkle sugar over butter. Arrange pears in pan; bake 10 minutes.

3 Meanwhile, combine flour, baking powder, cinnamon, baking soda and salt in small bowl; set aside. Combine milk, egg, fruit spread, oil and ginger in medium bowl; mix well. Add flour mixture; stir until well mixed. (Batter will be very thick.) Carefully spread batter evenly over pears to edge of pan.

4 Bake 20 to 25 minutes or until golden brown and toothpick inserted into center comes out clean.

5 Cool 5 minutes in pan on wire rack. Use knife to loosen cake from side of pan. Place 10-inch plate over top of pan; quickly invert cake onto plate. Place any pears left in pan on top of cake. Serve warm.   *Makes 8 servings*

Calories: 139 (27% of calories from fat), Total Fat: 4g, Saturated Fat: 1g, Carbohydrate: 23g, Cholesterol: 31mg, Protein: 3g, Sodium: 174mg, Dietary Fiber: 2g

Exchanges: 1 Starch, ½ Fat, ½ Fruit

Favorite Cookies

Reduced-Sugar Chocolate Chip **Cookies**

½ cup (1 stick) butter or margarine, softened

¼ cup granulated sugar

½ cup measure-for-measure sugar substitute

1 egg

1 teaspoon vanilla extract

1 cup all-purpose flour

3 tablespoons HERSHEY'S Cocoa or HERSHEY'S SPECIAL DARK® Cocoa

½ teaspoon baking soda

⅛ teaspoon salt

2 tablespoons skim milk

⅓ cup HERSHEY'S MINI CHIPS™ Semi-Sweet Chocolate Chips

1 Heat oven to 375°F.

2 Beat butter, granulated sugar and sugar substitute with electric mixer on medium speed in medium bowl until well blended. Add egg and vanilla; beat well. Stir together flour, cocoa, baking soda and salt; add alternately with milk to butter mixture, beating until well blended. Stir in mini chocolate chips. Drop by teaspoons onto ungreased cookie sheet.

3 Bake 7 to 9 minutes or just until set. Remove to wire rack and cool completely.

Makes 3 dozen cookies (2 cookies per serving)

Calories: 107 (50% of calories from fat), Total Fat: 6g, Saturated Fat: 4g, Carbohydrate: 11g, Cholesterol: 25mg, Protein: 2g, Sodium: 57mg, Dietary Fiber: 1g

Exchanges: 1 Starch, 1 Fat

CHOCOLATE CHIP DOUGH

⅓ cup stick butter or
    margarine, softened

1 egg

1 teaspoon vanilla

⅓ cup EQUAL® SPOONFUL*

⅓ cup firmly packed brown
    sugar

1 cup all-purpose flour

½ teaspoon baking soda

¼ teaspoon salt

½ cup mini semi-sweet
    chocolate chips

FUDGE NUT FILLING

1 cup EQUAL®
    SPOONFUL**

¾ cup all-purpose flour

6 tablespoons
    unsweetened cocoa

⅓ cup chopped nuts

1 teaspoon baking powder

¼ teaspoon salt

½ cup unsweetened
    applesauce

6 tablespoons stick butter
    or margarine, softened

2 eggs

1 teaspoon vanilla

- For Chocolate Chip Dough, beat ⅓ cup butter with electric mixer until fluffy. Beat in 1 egg and 1 teaspoon vanilla until blended. Mix in ⅓ cup Equal® Spoonful and brown sugar until combined. Combine 1 cup flour, baking soda, and ¼ teaspoon salt. Mix into butter mixture.

- Stir in chocolate chips. Form dough into circle about ½ inch thick. Wrap tightly in plastic wrap and freeze while preparing Fudge Nut Filling.

- For Fudge Nut Filling, combine 1 cup Equal® Spoonful, ¾ cup flour, cocoa, nuts, baking powder and ¼ teaspoon salt. Beat applesauce, 6 tablespoons butter, 2 eggs and 1 teaspoon vanilla until blended. Stir in combined flour mixture until well blended.

- Remove Chocolate Chip Dough from freezer. Spread approximately 1 rounded tablespoonful of dough in each of 24 mini-muffin pans. Fill each with Fudge Nut Filling to top of cup.

- Bake in preheated 350°F oven 15 to 18 minutes. Let cool in muffin pans about 5 minutes; remove and cool completely on wire racks. Store in airtight container at room temperature.

Makes 2 dozen cookies (1 cookie per serving)

*May substitute 8 packets EQUAL® sweetener.

**May substitute 24 packets EQUAL® sweetener.

Calories: 140 (51% of calories from fat), Total Fat: 8g, Saturated Fat: 5g, Carbohydrate: 15g, Cholesterol: 41mg, Protein: 3g, Sodium: 145mg, Dietary Fiber: 1g

Exchanges: 1 Starch, 1½ Fat

Light Latte **Cookies**

COOKIES

1¾ cups all-purpose flour

¼ cup unsweetened cocoa powder

1 tablespoons instant coffee granules

1 teaspoon baking soda

½ teaspoon ground cinnamon

½ cup (1 stick) soft baking butter with canola oil

½ cup packed dark brown sugar

¼ cup fat-free sour cream

1 egg

1 egg white

1 teaspoon vanilla

1 tablespoon powdered sugar (optional)

ICING

2 tablespoons fat-free half-and-half

¼ cup chopped bittersweet chocolate

1 teaspoon instant coffee granules

1 Preheat oven to 350°F. Combine flour, cocoa, coffee granules, baking soda and cinnamon in medium bowl; set aside.

2 Beat butter 30 seconds on medium speed of electric mixture until creamy. Beat in brown sugar and sour cream on medium-low speed until well blended. Add egg, egg white and vanilla; beat on low speed until well blended.

3 Gradually add flour mixture to butter mixture, beating on low speed until well blended.

4 Drop dough by level teaspoonfuls onto ungreased cookie sheets. Flatten dough slightly with bottom of greased drinking glass. Bake 6 minutes. Cool 5 minutes on cookie sheets; remove to wire rack to cool completely. Lightly dust cookies with powdered sugar, if desired.

5 For icing, heat half-and-half in small saucepan over low heat. Add chocolate and coffee granules, stirring until chocolate melts. Cool slightly.

6 Drizzle icing over cookies. Cool until icing hardens.

Makes 72 cookies (3 cookies per serving)

Calories: 102 (40% of calories from fat), Total Fat: 6g, Saturated Fat: 2g, Carbohydrate: 15g, Cholesterol: 3mg, Protein: 3g, Sodium: 114mg, Dietary Fiber: 2g

Exchanges: 1 Starch, 1 Fat

1¾ cups all-purpose flour

¼ cup unprocessed bran

½ teaspoon baking soda

⅛ teaspoon salt

**½ cup (1 stick) soft baking
  butter with canola oil**

¼ cup sugar

**¼ cup unsweetened
  applesauce**

1 egg white

1 teaspoon vanilla

**2 tablespoons plus
  ½ teaspoon red or green
  fine decorating sugar**

1 Combine flour, bran, baking soda and salt in medium bowl; set aside.

2 Beat butter and sugar 1 minute in large bowl on medium speed of electric mix or until creamy. Add applesauce, egg white and vanilla; beat on low speed until just blended. Beat 1 minute on medium or until smooth.

3 Gradually add flour mixture to butter mixture, beating on low speed until well blended. Divide dough into 2 portions. Roll each portion into 11-inch log. Wrap in plastic wrap; freeze at least 1 hour.

4 Preheat oven to 350°F.

5 Remove logs from freezer. Cut logs into ¼-inch slices, turning the log a little after each slice to keep it round.

6 Dip half of one side of each cookie into decorating sugar. Place cookies, sugar side up, on ungreased cookie sheet. Bake 6 to 8 minutes or until set. Cool 2 minutes on cookie sheet. Remove to wire rack to cool completely.

Makes 68 cookies (4 cookies per serving)

Calories: 120 (60% of calories from fat), Total Fat: 8g, Saturated Fat: 3g, Carbohydrate: 16g, Cholesterol: 12mg, Protein: 3g, Sodium: 132mg, Dietary Fiber: 3g

Exchanges: 1 Starch, 1 Fat

2 cups all-purpose flour

1½ teaspoons ground ginger

1 teaspoon baking soda

¼ teaspoon salt

¼ teaspoon ground cinnamon

¼ teaspoon ground cloves

¼ cup packed brown sugar

¼ cup canola oil

¼ cup molasses

½ cup fat-free sour cream

1 egg white

1 Preheat oven to 350°F. Combine flour, ginger, baking soda, salt, cinnamon and cloves in medium bowl; set aside.

2 Beat brown sugar, oil and molasses 1 minute in large bowl at medium speed of electric mixer or until smooth. Beat in sour cream and egg white until well blended.

3 Gradually add flour mixture to sugar mixture, beating on low speed until well blended.

4 Drop dough by level tablespoonfuls 2 inches apart onto ungreased cookie sheets. Flatten dough to ⅛-inch thickness with bottom of glass lightly sprayed with nonstick cooking spray.

5 Bake 10 minutes or until tops of cookies puff up and spring back when lightly touched. Cool 2 minutes on cookie sheets. Remove to wire racks to cool completely.

Makes 33 cookies (1 cookie per serving)

Calories: 60 (30% of calories from fat), Total Fat: 2g, Saturated Fat: <1g, Carbohydrate: 10g, Cholesterol: <1mg, Protein: 1g, Sodium: 65mg, Dietary Fiber: <1g

Exchanges: ½ Starch, ½ Fat

1 Preheat oven to 350°F. Combine flour, baking soda and salt in medium bowl; set aside.

2 Place dates and water in small covered saucepan; bring water to a boil over high heat. Reduce heat to medium; simmer about 1 minute or until dates soften. Place dates and cooking liquid in blender or food processor. Process using on/off pulsing action until mixture becomes pasty.

3 Melt butter and chocolate in small pan over very low heat, stirring constantly. Remove from heat; cool slightly.

4 Beat date paste, chocolate mixture, brown sugar and sour cream 1 minute in large bowl on medium speed of electric mixer until well blended.

5 Gradually beat in flour mixture on low speed until well blended.

6 Drop dough by level teaspoonfuls onto ungreased nonstick cookie sheets. Sprinkle cocoa lightly over tops of cookies using small mesh sieve. Bake cookies 6 minutes or until just set. *Do not overbake.* Cool cookies 2 minutes on cookie sheets on wire rack. Remove to wire rack to cool completely.

Makes 72 cookies (4 cookies per serving)

1½ cups all-purpose flour

½ teaspoon baking soda

⅛ teaspoon salt

10 pitted dates, chopped

½ cup water

¼ cup (½ stick) soft baking butter with canola oil

¼ cup chopped bittersweet chocolate

¼ cup dark brown sugar

¼ cup fat-free sour cream

1 tablespoon unsweetened cocoa powder

Calories: 100 (30% of calories from fat), Total Fat: 4g, Saturated Fat: 3g, Carbohydrate: 20g, Cholesterol: 8mg, Protein: 3g, Sodium: 76mg, Dietary Fiber: 3g

Exchanges: 1 Starch, ½ Fat

1¼ cups chopped apples

½ cup dried cranberries

½ cup reduced-fat sour cream

¼ cup cholesterol-free egg substitute

¼ cup (½ stick) margarine or butter, melted

3 tablespoons sugar, divided

1 package quick-rise active dry yeast

1 teaspoon vanilla

2 cups all-purpose flour

1 teaspoon ground cinnamon

1 tablespoon reduced-fat (2%) milk

1 Preheat oven to 350°F. Lightly coat cookie sheets with nonstick cooking spray.

2 Place apples and cranberries in food processor or blender; process with on/off pulsing action until finely chopped. Set aside.

3 Combine sour cream, egg substitute, margarine and 2 tablespoons sugar in medium bowl. Add yeast and vanilla. Add flour; stir to form ball. Turn dough out onto lightly floured work surface. Knead 1 minute. Cover with plastic wrap; let stand 10 minutes.

4 Divide dough into thirds. Roll one portion into 12-inch circle. Spread with ⅓ apple mixture (about ¼ cup). Cut dough to make 8 wedges. Roll up each wedge, beginning at outside edge. Place on prepared baking sheet; turn ends of cookies to form crescents. Repeat with remaining dough and apple mixture.

5 Combine remaining 1 tablespoon sugar and cinnamon in small bowl. Lightly brush cookies with milk; sprinkle with sugar-cinnamon mixture. Bake 18 to 20 minutes or until lightly browned.   *Makes 2 dozen cookies*

Calories: 82 (22% of calories from fat), Total Fat: 2g, Saturated Fat: 1g, Carbohydrate: 13g, Cholesterol: 2mg, Protein: 2g, Sodium: 31mg, Dietary Fiber: 1g

Exchanges: 1 Starch

Pistachio **Pinwheels**

1 package (8 ounces)
    reduced-fat cream
    cheese, softened

½ cup (1 stick) soft baking
    butter with canola oil

2 cups all-purpose flour

3 tablespoons apricot fruit
    spread

1 tablespoon water

2 tablespoons sugar

¼ teaspoon ground
    cinnamon

½ cup finely chopped
    toasted pistachio nuts

Nonstick cooking spray

Additional apricot fruit
    spread, melted
    (optional)

1 Preheat oven to 350°F. Line cookie sheets with parchment paper; set aside. Beat cream cheese and butter 1 minute in large bowl on medium speed of electric mixer until creamy.

2 Add flour to cream cheese mixture in 3 batches, beating well on low speed after each addition.

3 Divide dough into two equal portions. Shape each portion into a rectangle. Wrap in plastic wrap; refrigerate 20 minutes.

4 Mix 3 tablespoons fruit spread and water in small bowl until blended; set aside. In separate small bowl, mix sugar and cinnamon; set aside.

5 Remove one portion dough from refrigerator. Place on surface lightly dusted with flour. Roll dough out into 12×10-inch rectangle.

6 Spread 2 tablespoons fruit spread mixture onto dough. Sprinkle 1½ teaspoons cinnamon-sugar mixture evenly over fruit spread mixture. Sprinkle with ¼ cup pistachio nuts.

7 Cut dough in half lengthwise into two 12×5-inch rectangles. Roll up rectangle jelly-roll fashion, starting with long side, to form 12-inch long roll. Repeat with remaining dough, fruit spread mixture, cinnamon-sugar mixture and nuts.

8 Cut each roll into 16 (¾-inch-thick) slices. Place cookies on prepared cookie sheets. Spray tops of cookies with cooking spay; sprinkle with remaining cinnamon-sugar mixture.

9 Bake 16 minutes or until golden. Cool 2 minutes on cookie sheets. Remove to wire racks. Melt additional fruit spread in small saucepan over low heat, if desired. Brush onto cookies. *Makes 64 cookies (2 cookies per serving)*

Calories: 90 (60% of calories from fat), Total Fat: 6g, Saturated Fat: 1g, Carbohydrate: 10g, Cholesterol: 6mg, Protein: 2g, Sodium: 68mg, Dietary Fiber: 1g

Exchanges: ½ Starch, 1 Fat

Double Chocolate Biscotti

¾ **cup all-purpose flour**

3 **tablespoons sugar**
   substitute

3 **tablespoons packed**
   brown sugar

2 **tablespoons**
   unsweetened cocoa

1 **teaspoon baking powder**

¼ **teaspoon salt**

2 **tablespoons butter**

2 **egg whites, lightly**
   beaten

1 **tablespoon chocolate**
   syrup

½ **cup puffed wheat cereal**

4 **teaspoons sliced almonds**

1 Preheat oven to 350°F. Line cookie sheet with parchment paper; set aside.

2 Combine flour, sugar substitute, brown sugar, cocoa, baking powder and salt in medium bowl; set aside.

3 Melt butter in small saucepan over low heat. Pour into small bowl; cool slightly. Stir in egg whites and chocolate syrup. Stir butter mixture into flour mixture until stiff dough forms. Stir in cereal.

4 Turn dough out onto cookie sheet; shape dough into log 12 inches long log and 2 inches wide. Press almonds onto log. Bake 20 to 25 minutes or until firm.

5 Cool completely on wire rack. *Reduce oven temperature to 300°F.*

6 Using serrated knife, cut loaf into ½-inch-thick diagonal slices. Place slices, cut sides down, onto cookie sheet. Bake 10 minutes. Turn over biscotti slices. Bake 10 minutes more. Cool completely on wire rack.

Makes 24 cookies (2 cookies per serving)

Calories: 76 (47% of calories from fat), Total Fat: 4g, Saturated Fat: 1g, Carbohydrate: 12g, Cholesterol: 6mg, Protein: 2g, Sodium: 116mg, Dietary Fiber: 1g

Exchanges: ½ Starch, ½ Fat

Easy Bars
& Brownies

PM Snack Bars

3 tablespoons creamy peanut butter

2 tablespoons molasses

2 egg whites

2 tablespoons ground flaxseed

4 cups crisp rice cereal

½ cup sliced almonds

1 ounce bittersweet chocolate, melted and cooled

1 Preheat oven to 350°F. Place peanut butter in small microwavable bowl; microwave 30 seconds on LOW (30% power) or until peanut butter is melted. Stir in molasses; cool.

2 Place egg whites in blender with flaxseed. Process until foamy. Pour into large bowl. Add peanut butter mixture; stir until smooth. Stir in cereal and almonds until cereal is evenly coated.

3 Spray 9×9 baking pan with nonstick cooking spray. Press cereal mixture into pan. Bake 20 to 25 minutes or until browned on top. Cool completely in pan on wire rack. Drizzle melted chocolate over bars. Cut into 16 bars.

Makes 16 servings (2¼-inch square per serving)

Calories: 91 (41% of calories from fat), Total Fat: 4g, Saturated Fat: 1g, Carbohydrate: 11g, Cholesterol: <1mg, Protein: 3g, Sodium: 24mg, Dietary Fiber: 1g

Exchanges: ½ Starch, 1 Fat

¾ **cup all-purpose flour**

½ **cup packed brown sugar**

½ **cup uncooked quick oats**

¼ **cup toasted wheat germ**

¼ **cup unsweetened applesauce**

¼ **cup margarine or butter, softened**

⅛ **teaspoon salt**

½ **cup cholesterol-free egg substitute**

¼ **cup raisins**

¼ **cup dried cranberries**

¼ **cup sunflower kernels**

1 **tablespoon grated orange peel**

1 **teaspoon ground cinnamon**

1 Preheat oven to 350°F. Lightly coat 13×9-inch baking pan with nonstick cooking spray; set aside.

2 Beat flour, sugar, oats, wheat germ, applesauce, margarine and salt in large bowl with electric mixer at medium speed until well blended. Add egg substitute, raisins, cranberries, sunflower kernels, orange peel and cinnamon. Spread into pan.

3 Bake 15 minutes or until firm to touch. Cool completely in pan on wire rack. Cut into 24 squares.

Makes 24 servings

Calories: 80 (33% of calories from fat), Total Fat: 3g, Saturated Fat: <1g, Carbohydrate: 12g, Cholesterol: 0mg, Protein: 2g, Sodium: 46mg, Dietary Fiber: 1g

Exchanges: 1 Starch, ½ Fat

1 cup EQUAL® SPOONFUL*

¾ cup all-purpose flour

½ cup semi-sweet
chocolate chips or
mini chocolate chips

6 tablespoons
unsweetened cocoa

1 teaspoon baking powder

¼ teaspoon salt

6 tablespoons stick butter
or margarine, softened

½ cup unsweetened
applesauce

2 eggs

1 teaspoon vanilla

- Combine Equal®, flour, chocolate chips, cocoa, baking powder and salt. Beat butter, applesauce, eggs and vanilla until blended. Stir in combined flour mixture until blended.

- Spread batter in 8-inch square baking pan sprayed with nonstick cooking spray. Bake in preheated 350°F oven 18 to 20 minutes or until top springs back when gently touched. Cool completely in pan on wire rack.   *Makes 16 servings*

May substitute 24 packets EQUAL® sweetener.

Calories: 108 (58% of calories from fat), Total Fat: 7g, Saturated Fat: 4g, Carbohydrate: 10g, Cholesterol: 38mg, Protein: 2g, Sodium: 119mg, Dietary Fiber: 1g

Exchanges: 1 Starch, 1 Fat

No-Guilt Chocolate Brownies

1 cup semisweet
   chocolate chips

¼ cup packed brown sugar

2 tablespoons granulated
   sugar

½ teaspoon baking powder

¼ teaspoon salt

½ cup cholesterol-free egg
   substitute

1 jar (2½ ounces) first-stage
   baby food prunes

1 teaspoon vanilla

1 cup uncooked
   old-fashioned oats

⅓ cup nonfat dry milk
   powder

¼ cup wheat germ

2 teaspoons powdered
   sugar

1 Preheat oven to 350°F. Spray 8-inch square baking pan with nonstick cooking spray; set aside. Melt chips in top of double boiler over simmering water.

2 Combine brown and granulated sugars, baking powder and salt in large bowl. Add egg substitute, prunes and vanilla; beat 2 minutes with electric mixer at medium speed until well blended. Stir in oats, dry milk, wheat germ and chocolate.

3 Pour batter into prepared pan. Bake 30 minutes or until toothpick inserted in center comes out clean. Cool completely in pan on wire rack. Cut into 16 (2-inch) squares. Dust with powdered sugar before serving.

Makes 16 servings

Calories: 124 (36% of calories from fat), Total Fat: 5g, Saturated Fat: <1g, Carbohydrate: 21g, Cholesterol: <1mg, Protein: 3g, Sodium: 65mg, Dietary Fiber: <1g

Exchanges: 1 Starch, 1 Fat

1 Preheat oven to 350°F.

2 Combine flour, 12 packets sugar substitute, cocoa, baking powder and salt in large bowl; stir until well blended. Combine prune purée, coffee, egg, oil and ½ teaspoon vanilla in medium bowl; stir until well blended. Make well in center of dry ingredients; add prune mixture. Stir until just blended.

3 Spread batter evenly in ungreased 8×8-inch nonstick baking pan. Bake 8 minutes. (Brownies will not appear to be done.) Cool completely in pan on wire rack.

4 Meanwhile, place raspberry spread in small microwavable bowl. Microwave on HIGH 10 seconds; stir until smooth. Brush evenly over brownies with pastry brush.

5 Combine cream cheese, 4½ teaspoons milk, remaining 2 packets sugar substitute and remaining ¼ teaspoon vanilla in medium bowl. Beat at medium speed of electric mixer until well blended and smooth.

6 To serve, cut brownies into 12 rectangles; top each brownie with 1 teaspoon cream cheese mixture.

Makes 12 servings

*This recipe was tested with aspartame-based sugar substitute.

¾ **cup all-purpose flour**

14 packets sugar substitute,* divided

¼ **cup unsweetened cocoa powder**

¾ **teaspoon baking powder**

⅛ **teaspoon salt**

1 **jar (2½ ounces) prune purée**

¼ **cup cold coffee or fat-free (skim) milk**

1 **egg**

2 **tablespoons canola oil**

¾ **teaspoon vanilla, divided**

¼ **cup seedless raspberry fruit spread**

2 **ounces reduced-fat cream cheese**

4½ **teaspoons fat-free (skim) milk**

Calories: 89 (30% of calories from fat), Total Fat: 3g, Saturated Fat: <1g, Carbohydrate: 12g, Cholesterol: 2mg, Protein: 2g, Sodium: 93mg, Dietary Fiber: <1g

Exchanges: 1 Starch, ½ Fat

Cheery Cherry **Brownies**

¾ **cup all-purpose flour**

½ **cup sugar substitute**

½ **cup unsweetened cocoa
     powder**

¼ **teaspoon baking soda**

½ **cup evaporated
     skimmed milk**

⅓ **cup butter, melted**

¼ **cup cholesterol-free egg
     substitute**

¼ **cup honey**

 1 **teaspoon vanilla**

½ **(15½-ounce) can pitted
     tart red cherries,
     drained and halved**

1 Preheat oven to 350°F. Grease 11×7-inch baking pan; set aside.

2 Stir together flour, sugar substitute, cocoa and baking soda in large mixing bowl. Add milk, butter, egg substitute, honey and vanilla. Stir just until blended.

3 Pour into prepared pan. Sprinkle cherries over top of chocolate mixture. Bake 13 to 15 minutes or until toothpick inserted into center comes out clean. Cool completely in pan on wire rack. Cut into 12 brownies.

Makes 12 servings

Calories: 130 (41% of calories from fat), Total Fat: 6g, Saturated Fat: 4g, Carbohydrate: 18g, Cholesterol: 28mg, Protein: 3g, Sodium: 110mg, Dietary Fiber: 2g

Exchanges: 1 Starch, 1 Fat

1 cup EQUAL® SPOONFUL*

½ cup stick butter or
   margarine, softened

⅓ cup firmly packed brown
   sugar

½ cup 2% milk

½ cup creamy peanut butter

1 egg

1 teaspoon vanilla

1 cup all-purpose flour

¾ cup quick oats, uncooked

½ teaspoon baking soda

¼ teaspoon salt

¾ cup mini semi-sweet
   chocolate chips

- Beat Equal®, butter and brown sugar until well combined. Stir in milk, peanut butter, egg and vanilla until blended. Gradually mix in combined flour, oats, baking soda and salt until blended. Stir in chocolate chips.

- Spread mixture evenly in 13×9-inch baking pan generously coated with nonstick cooking spray. Bake in preheated 350°F oven 20 to 22 minutes. Cool completely in pan on wire rack. Cut into squares; store in airtight container at room temperature.   *Makes 48 bars*

May substitute 24 packets EQUAL® sweetener.

Calories: 68 (53% of calories from fat), Total Fat: 4g, Saturated Fat: 2g, Carbohydrate: 7g, Cholesterol: 10mg, Protein: 1g, Sodium: 60mg, Dietary Fiber: 1g

Exchanges: ½ Starch, 1 Fat

Marvelous **Muffins**

Blueberry-Orange **Muffins**

1¾ cups all-purpose flour

⅓ cup sugar

2½ teaspoons baking powder

½ teaspoon baking soda

½ teaspoon salt

½ teaspoon ground
cinnamon

¾ cup fat-free (skim) milk

1 egg, lightly beaten

¼ cup butter, melted and
slightly cooled

3 tablespoons orange
juice concentrate,
thawed

1 teaspoon vanilla

¾ cup fresh or frozen
blueberries, thawed

1 Preheat oven to 400°F. Grease or line 12 (2½-inch) muffin pan cups with paper liners; set aside.

2 Combine flour, sugar, baking powder, baking soda, salt and cinnamon in large bowl. Beat milk, egg, butter, orange juice concentrate and vanilla in medium bowl until well blended. Add milk mixture to flour mixture; stir just until dry ingredients are barely moistened (mixture will be lumpy). Stir in blueberries just until evenly distributed.

3 Fill prepared muffin cups ¾ full. Bake 20 to 25 minutes (25 to 30 minutes if using frozen berries) or until toothpick inserted into centers comes out clean. Cool 5 minutes in pan; remove muffins to wire rack. Serve warm.

Makes 12 servings

Calories: 149 (28% of calories from fat), Total Fat: 5g, Saturated Fat: 3g, Carbohydrate: 24g, Cholesterol: 29mg, Protein: 3g, Sodium: 307mg, Dietary Fiber: 1g

Exchanges: 1½ Starch, 1 Fat

Cranberry Sunshine **Muffins**

1½ cups all-purpose flour

½ cup **SPLENDA®**
No Calorie Sweetener,
Granular

2 teaspoons baking powder

1 teaspoon baking soda

½ teaspoon ground
cinnamon

1 cup chopped fresh or
frozen cranberries

¼ cup chopped walnuts

½ cup orange juice

¼ cup nonfat sour cream

1 egg or equivalent in egg
substitute

1 tablespoon plus
1 teaspoon reduced-
calorie margarine

1 Preheat oven to 375°F. Spray 8 muffin pan cups with butter-flavored cooking spray or line with paper liners.

2 In large bowl, combine flour, SPLENDA®, baking powder, baking soda and cinnamon. Stir in cranberries and walnuts.

3 In small bowl, combine orange juice, sour cream, egg, and margarine. Add liquid mixture to dry mixture. Stir gently just to combine. Evenly spoon batter into prepared muffin cups.

4 Bake for 15 to 20 minutes or until toothpick inserted into centers comes out clean. Cool in pan on wire rack for 5 minutes. Remove muffins from pan and continue cooling on wire rack.   *Makes 8 servings*

HINT: Fill unused muffin cups with water. It protects the muffin pan and ensures even baking.

Calories: 156 (25% of calories from fat), Total Fat: 4g, Saturated Fat: 1g, Carbohydrate: 25g, Cholesterol: 27mg, Protein: 4g, Sodium: 318mg, Dietary Fiber: 2g

Exchanges: 1½ Starch, 1 Fat

¾ **cup less 2 tablespoons all-purpose flour**

⅜ **cup sugar substitute***

½ **teaspoon baking powder**

½ **teaspoon ground cinnamon**

¼ **teaspoon baking soda**

½ **cup egg substitute**

2 **tablespoons unsweetened applesauce**

1 **tablespoon canola oil**

½ **teaspoon vanilla**

1 **cup shredded carrots**

2 **tablespoons raisins**

1 Preheat oven to 400°F. Lightly spray 2 (8-ounce) ovenproof coffee cups with nonstick cooking spray; set aside.

2 Combine flour, sugar substitute, baking powder, cinnamon and baking soda in medium bowl.

3 Whisk together egg substitute, applesauce, oil and vanilla in another medium bowl about 1 minute or until smooth. Add carrots and raisins; stir until well blended. Add flour mixture to egg mixture; stir about 1 minute or just until smooth.

4 Spoon batter into prepared coffee cups. Push shredded carrots into batter to smooth tops.

5 Place cups on baking sheet; bake 20 minutes on center oven rack or until toothpick inserted into centers comes out clean.

6 Cool 5 minutes. Serve in cup or run knife around edges to loosen and slide out onto serving plate.

Makes 2 servings

*This recipe was tested with sucralose-based sugar substitute.

Calories: 317 (21% of calories from fat), Total Fat: 7g, Saturated Fat: <1g, Carbohydrate: 52g, Cholesterol: 0mg, Protein: 11g, Sodium: 442mg, Dietary Fiber: 4g

Exchanges: 3 Starch, ½ Fruit, 1½ Fat

Apricot-Pecan Bran **Muffins**

⅓ cup pecan chips

⅓ cup plus 1 tablespoon
   sugar, divided

1 cup extra-fiber bran
   cereal

1 cup low-fat buttermilk

4 ounces baby food puréed
   prunes

½ cup chopped dried
   apricots or golden
   raisins

2 egg whites

2 teaspoons vanilla

1 cup all-purpose flour

2 teaspoons baking powder

1 teaspoon ground
   cinnamon

¼ teaspoon salt

1 Preheat oven to 400°F. Line 12 (2½-inch) muffin pan cups with paper baking cups; set aside. Combine pecans and 1 tablespoon sugar in small bowl; set aside.

2 Combine cereal, buttermilk, prunes, apricots, egg whites and vanilla in medium bowl; stir to coat completely. Let stand 5 minutes.

3 Meanwhile, combine flour, remaining ⅓ cup sugar, baking powder, cinnamon and salt in large mixing bowl. Make a well in center of flour mixture; add buttermilk mixture. Stir just until blended.

4 Spoon batter into prepared muffin cups. Sprinkle evenly with pecan mixture. Bake 20 minutes or until toothpick inserted into centers comes out clean. Cool in pan on wire rack 5 minutes. Remove from pan to wire rack. Serve warm or at room temperature.   *Makes 12 servings*

Calories: 129 (21% of calories from fat), Total Fat: 3g, Saturated Fat: <1g, Carbohydrate: 26g, Cholesterol: <1mg, Protein: 4g, Sodium: 193mg, Dietary Fiber: 4g

Exchanges: 1 Starch, ½ Fruit, ½ Fat

¾ **cup canned pumpkin**

6 **tablespoons vegetable oil**

1 **egg**

2 **egg whites**

1 **tablespoon light molasses**

1 **teaspoon vanilla**

1¼ **cups all-purpose flour**

1 **cup EQUAL® SPOONFUL***

½ **cup raisins**

1 **tablespoon baking powder**

1 **teaspoon ground cinnamon**

½ **teaspoon ground nutmeg**

½ **teaspoon ground ginger**

¼ **teaspoon salt**

- Combine pumpkin, oil, egg and egg whites, molasses and vanilla. Stir in combined flour, Equal®, raisins, baking powder, cinnamon, nutmeg, ginger and salt just until all ingredients are moistened. Fill paper-lined 2½-inch muffin cups about ¾ full.

- Bake in preheated 375°F oven 18 to 20 minutes or until wooden pick inserted into centers comes out clean. Cool in pan on wire rack 2 to 3 minutes. Remove muffins from pan and cool completely on wire rack.   *Makes 12 muffins*

*May substitute 24 packets EQUAL® sweetener.

Calories: 149 (48% of calories from fat), Total Fat: 8g, Saturated Fat: 1g, Carbohydrate: 18g, Cholesterol: 18mg, Protein: 3g, Sodium: 224mg, Dietary Fiber: 1g

Exchanges: 1 Starch, 1½ Fat

8 tablespoons sugar, divided

2½ to 3 teaspoons ground cinnamon, divided

1 cup 100% bran cereal

1 cup fat-free (skim) milk

1 cup all-purpose flour

1 tablespoon baking powder

½ teaspoon baking soda

½ teaspoon salt

1 cup solid-pack pumpkin

1 egg, beaten

1 tablespoon vanilla

1 package (2 ounces) pecan chips (½ cup)

1 Preheat oven to 400°F. Spray 12 (2½-inch) nonstick muffin pan cups with nonstick cooking spray; set aside. Combine 2 tablespoons sugar and ½ to 1 teaspoon cinnamon in small bowl for topping; set aside.

2 Blend cereal and milk in large bowl; set aside 5 minutes to soften. Meanwhile, combine flour, remaining 6 tablespoons sugar, remaining cinnamon, baking powder, baking soda and salt in large bowl; mix well.

3 Whisk pumpkin, egg and vanilla into cereal mixture. Gently fold in flour mixture just until blended. *Do not overmix.* Spoon equal amounts of batter into prepared muffin cups; sprinkle evenly with pecan chips. Sprinkle with cinnamon-sugar topping.

4 Bake 20 to 25 minutes or until toothpick inserted into centers comes out clean. Cool on wire rack 3 minutes before removing muffins from pan. Serve warm or at room temperature. *Makes 12 servings*

Calories: 141 (25% of calories from fat), Total Fat: 4g, Saturated Fat: <1g, Carbohydrate: 24g, Cholesterol: 18mg, Protein: 4g, Sodium: 335mg, Dietary Fiber: 3g

Exchanges: 1½ Starch, 1 Fat

1 cup all-purpose flour

1 cup uncooked
old-fashioned oats

¼ cup packed brown sugar

1 teaspoon baking powder

1 teaspoon baking soda

¾ teaspoon ground
cinnamon, divided

¼ teaspoon salt

8 ounces lemon-flavored
nonfat yogurt

¼ cup cholesterol-free egg
substitute *or* 2 egg
whites

1 tablespoon vegetable oil

1 teaspoon grated
lemon peel

1 teaspoon vanilla

1 cup fresh or frozen
blueberries

1 tablespoon granulated
sugar

1 tablespoon sliced
almonds (optional)

1 Preheat oven to 400°F. Spray 12 (2½-inch) muffin cups with nonstick cooking spray; set aside.

2 Combine flour, oats, brown sugar, baking powder, baking soda, ½ teaspoon cinnamon and salt in large bowl.

3 Combine yogurt, egg substitute, oil, lemon peel and vanilla in small bowl; stir into flour mixture just until blended. Gently stir in blueberries. Spoon mixture into prepared muffin cups.

4 Mix granulated sugar, remaining ¼ teaspoon cinnamon and almonds, if desired, in small bowl. Sprinkle over muffin mixture.

5 Bake 18 to 20 minutes or until lightly browned and toothpick inserted into centers comes out clean. Cool slightly before serving.   *Makes 12 servings*

Calories: 125 (14% of calories from fat), Total Fat: 2g, Saturated Fat: 0g, Carbohydrate: 24g, Cholesterol: 1mg, Protein: 3g, Sodium: 198mg, Dietary Fiber: 1g

Exchanges: 1½ Starch

BATTER

2 cups all-purpose flour

1 cup EQUAL® Sugar Lite™

½ teaspoon ground cinnamon

½ teaspoon baking soda

½ teaspoon salt

1 cup buttermilk

¼ cup butter, melted and cooled to lukewarm

1 egg

1 teaspoon vanilla extract

1 cup chopped fresh cranberries

1 tablespoon grated orange peel

TOPPING

2 tablespoons EQUAL® Sugar Lite™

¼ teaspoon ground cinnamon

Combine flour, 1 cup EQUAL® Sugar Lite™, ½ teaspoon cinnamon, baking soda and salt. Stir in buttermilk, melted butter, egg and vanilla just until combined. Fold in cranberries and orange peel until blended.

To make topping, combine 2 tablespoons EQUAL® Sugar Lite™ and ¼ teaspoon cinnamon. Preheat oven to 375°F.

Line a muffin pan with 2½-inch paper cups. Fill cups about two-thirds full with batter. Sprinkle topping mixture evenly over 12 filled cups. Bake 19 to 22 minutes or until wooden pick inserted near center comes out clean. Cool on wire rack. Serve warm or at room temperature.

Makes 12 muffins

NOTE: Muffins keep 1 to 2 days at room temperature, or up to 2 weeks frozen. To freeze, wrap them tightly in plastic wrap and place them in a freezer-safe, resealable container.

Calories: 164 (27% of calories from fat), Total Fat: 5g, Saturated Fat: 3g, Carbohydrate: 26g, Cholesterol: 29mg, Protein: 3g, Sodium: 206mg, Dietary Fiber: 1g

Exchanges: 1½ Starch, 1 Fat

Quick & Tasty Breads

Blueberry Walnut Coffee **Cake**

Prep Time: 10 minutes
Bake Time: 30 minutes

1¼ cups all-purpose flour

⅓ cup sugar substitute*

3 tablespoons granulated sugar

½ teaspoon grated lemon peel

½ teaspoon baking powder

½ teaspoon baking soda

¼ teaspoon salt

⅛ teaspoon ground nutmeg

⅔ cup low-fat buttermilk

¼ cup cholesterol-free egg substitute

2 tablespoons canola oil

1 cup fresh blueberries

3 tablespoons chopped walnuts

1 teaspoon powdered sugar

1 Preheat oven to 350°F. Lightly coat 9-inch round baking pan with nonstick cooking spray; set aside.

2 Combine flour, sugar substitute, granulated sugar, lemon peel, baking powder, baking soda, salt and nutmeg in large bowl.

3 Combine buttermilk, egg substitute and oil in small bowl. Stir into flour mixture just until moistened.

4 Gently fold in blueberries. Spread in prepared pan. Sprinkle with walnuts. Bake 30 to 35 minutes or until toothpick inserted into center comes out clean. Remove to wire rack. Cool 10 minutes. Sprinkle with powdered sugar. Serve warm. *Makes 8 servings*

This recipe was tested with sucralose-based sugar substitute.

Calories: 179 (30% of calories from fat), Total Fat: 6g, Saturated Fat: 1g, Carbohydrate: 32g, Cholesterol: 1mg, Protein: 4g, Sodium: 213mg, Dietary Fiber: 1g

Exchanges: 2 Starch, 1 Fat

Prep Time: 10 minutes

¼ **cup raisins or dried cranberries**

½ **cup water**

1 **package (11 ounces) refrigerated French bread dough**

1 **tablespoon granulated sugar**

1 **tablespoon sugar substitute***

1 **teaspoon ground cinnamon**

¼ **teaspoon ground nutmeg**

2 **tablespoons apricot fruit spread**

1 **ounce sliced almonds or pecan chips, toasted****

1 Preheat oven to 350° F.

2 Place raisins in small microwavable bowl; cover with water. Microwave at HIGH 2 minutes.

3 Unroll dough on work surface. Combine granulated sugar, sugar substitute, cinnamon and nutmeg in small bowl; stir until well blended. Sprinkle mixture evenly over dough.

4 Drain raisins; sprinkle evenly over sugar-cinnamon mixture. Roll up dough, starting at wide end.

5 Spray nonstick cookie sheet with nonstick cooking spray. Place dough on cookie sheet. Join two ends to make a ring. Pinch dough tightly to seal. Using serrated knife, make 5 to 6 diagonal slits on top of dough.

6 Bake 23 minutes or until golden. Remove to wire rack; let cool 5 minutes.

7 Place fruit spread in small microwavable bowl. Microwave on HIGH 15 seconds or until melted. Stir. Brush evenly over top and sides of coffee cake. Sprinkle with almonds. Cut into 8 slices. Serve warm or at room temperature.

Makes 8 servings

*This recipe was tested with sucralose-based sugar substitute.

**To toast almonds, spread in single layer on baking sheet. Bake in preheated 350°F oven 8 to 10 minutes or until golden brown, stirring frequently.

Calories: 148 (19% of calories from fat), Total Fat: 3g, Saturated Fat: 1g, Carbohydrate: 27g, Cholesterol: 0mg, Protein: 4g, Sodium: 247mg, Dietary Fiber: 2g

Peach-Almond Scones

2 cups all-purpose flour

¼ cup plus 1 tablespoon sugar, divided

2 teaspoons baking powder

½ teaspoon salt

5 tablespoons cold margarine or butter

½ cup sliced almonds, lightly toasted and divided

1 egg

2 tablespoons milk

1 can (16 ounces) peach halves or slices in juice, drained and finely chopped

½ teaspoon almond extract

1 Preheat oven to 425°F. Combine flour, ¼ cup sugar, baking powder and salt in large bowl. Cut in margarine with pastry blender or 2 knives until mixture resembles coarse crumbs. Stir in ¼ cup almonds. Lightly beat egg and milk in small bowl. Reserve 2 tablespoons egg mixture. Stir peaches and almond extract into remaining egg mixture. Stir into flour mixture until soft dough forms.

2 Place dough on well-floured surface. Gently knead 10 to 12 times. Roll dough into 9×6-inch rectangle. Cut into 6 (3-inch) squares using floured knife. Cut diagonally into halves, making 12 triangles; place 2 inches apart on ungreased baking sheets. Brush triangles with reserved egg mixture. Sprinkle with remaining ¼ cup almonds and 1 tablespoon sugar.

3 Bake 10 to 12 minutes or until golden brown. Remove from baking sheets and cool on wire racks 10 minutes. Serve warm. *Makes 12 scones*

SERVING SUGGESTION: Serve with butter or jelly, if desired.

Calories: 202 (36% of calories from fat), Total Fat: 8g, Saturated Fat: 1g, Carbohydrate: 27g, Cholesterol: 18mg, Protein: 4g, Sodium: 242mg, Dietary Fiber: 1g

Exchanges: 1½ Starch, ½ Fruit, 1½ Fat

⅓ **cup butter, softened**

1⅓ **cups EQUAL® Sugar Lite™**

¾ **cup canned pumpkin**

2 **eggs**

⅓ **cup 2% milk**

1 **teaspoon vanilla extract**

1½ **cups self-rising flour**

½ **teaspoon ground cinnamon**

½ **teaspoon ground nutmeg**

⅓ **cup raisins**

1½ **tablespoons self-rising flour**

Beat butter and EQUAL® Sugar Lite™ until well blended. Mix in pumpkin, eggs, milk and vanilla until combined.

Combine 1½ cups self-rising flour, cinnamon and nutmeg. Mix into pumpkin batter until well blended. Combine raisins and 1½ tablespoons flour. Fold into pumpkin mixture. Preheat oven to 350°F.

Spoon mixture into a 9×5×4-inch loaf pan well sprayed with cooking spray. Bake 50 to 55 minutes or until a wooden pick inserted near center comes out clean. Cool in pan on wire rack 10 minutes. Remove bread and cool completely. *Makes 16 servings*

Calories: 139 (32% of calories from fat), Total Fat: 5g, Saturated Fat: 3g, Carbohydrate: 21g, Cholesterol: 37mg, Protein: 2g, Sodium: 199mg, Dietary Fiber: 1g

Exchanges: 1½ Starch, 1 Fat

Brunch-Time Zucchini-Date **Bread**

BREAD

1 cup chopped pitted dates

1 cup water

1 cup whole wheat flour

1 cup all-purpose flour

2 tablespoons granulated sugar

1 teaspoon baking powder

½ teaspoon baking soda

½ teaspoon salt

½ teaspoon ground cinnamon

¼ teaspoon ground cloves

2 eggs

1 cup shredded zucchini, pressed dry with paper towels

CREAM CHEESE SPREAD

1 package (8 ounces) fat-free cream cheese

¼ cup powdered sugar

1 tablespoon vanilla

⅛ teaspoon ground cinnamon

Dash ground cloves

1 Preheat oven to 350°F. Spray 9×5-inch loaf pan with nonstick cooking spray; set aside.

2 For bread, combine dates and water in small saucepan. Bring to a boil over medium-high heat. Remove from heat; let stand 15 minutes.

3 Combine flours, granulated sugar, baking powder, baking soda, salt, cinnamon and cloves in large bowl. Beat eggs in medium bowl; stir in date mixture and zucchini. Stir egg mixture into flour mixture just until moistened. Pour batter evenly into prepared pan.

4 Bake 30 to 35 minutes or until toothpick inserted into center comes out clean. Cool 5 minutes. Remove from pan. Cool completely on wire rack.

5 Meanwhile, prepare cream cheese spread. Combine cream cheese, powdered sugar, vanilla, cinnamon and cloves in small bowl. Beat until smooth. Cover and refrigerate until ready to use.

6 Cut bread into 16 slices. Serve with cream cheese spread.

Makes 16 servings

Calories: 124 (7% of calories from fat), Total Fat: 1g, Saturated Fat: <1g, Carbohydrate: 24g, Cholesterol: 27mg, Protein: 5g, Sodium: 260mg, Dietary Fiber: 2g

Exchanges: 1½ Starch

The publisher would like to thank the companies and organizations listed below for the use of their recipes and photographs in this publication.

Equal® sweetener

The Hershey Company

Peanut Advisory Board

SPLENDA® is a trademark of McNeil Nutritionals, LLC

METRIC CONVERSION CHART

VOLUME MEASUREMENTS (dry)

$\frac{1}{8}$ teaspoon = 0.5 mL
$\frac{1}{4}$ teaspoon = 1 mL
$\frac{1}{2}$ teaspoon = 2 mL
$\frac{3}{4}$ teaspoon = 4 mL
1 teaspoon = 5 mL
1 tablespoon = 15 mL
2 tablespoons = 30 mL
$\frac{1}{4}$ cup = 60 mL
$\frac{1}{3}$ cup = 75 mL
$\frac{1}{2}$ cup = 125 mL
$\frac{2}{3}$ cup = 150 mL
$\frac{3}{4}$ cup = 175 mL
1 cup = 250 mL
2 cups = 1 pint = 500 mL
3 cups = 750 mL
4 cups = 1 quart = 1 L

VOLUME MEASUREMENTS (fluid)

1 fluid ounce (2 tablespoons) = 30 mL
4 fluid ounces ($\frac{1}{2}$ cup) = 125 mL
8 fluid ounces (1 cup) = 250 mL
12 fluid ounces (1$\frac{1}{2}$ cups) = 375 mL
16 fluid ounces (2 cups) = 500 mL

WEIGHTS (mass)

$\frac{1}{2}$ ounce = 15 g
1 ounce = 30 g
3 ounces = 90 g
4 ounces = 120 g
8 ounces = 225 g
10 ounces = 285 g
12 ounces = 360 g
16 ounces = 1 pound = 450 g

DIMENSIONS

$\frac{1}{16}$ inch = 2 mm
$\frac{1}{8}$ inch = 3 mm
$\frac{1}{4}$ inch = 6 mm
$\frac{1}{2}$ inch = 1.5 cm
$\frac{3}{4}$ inch = 2 cm
1 inch = 2.5 cm

OVEN TEMPERATURES

250°F = 120°C
275°F = 140°C
300°F = 150°C
325°F = 160°C
350°F = 180°C
375°F = 190°C
400°F = 200°C
425°F = 220°C
450°F = 230°C

BAKING PAN SIZES

Utensil	Size in Inches/Quarts	Metric Volume	Size in Centimeters
Baking or Cake Pan (square or rectangular)	8×8×2	2 L	20×20×5
	9×9×2	2.5 L	23×23×5
	12×8×2	3 L	30×20×5
	13×9×2	3.5 L	33×23×5
Loaf Pan	8×4×3	1.5 L	20×10×7
	9×5×3	2 L	23×13×7
Round Layer Cake Pan	8×1½	1.2 L	20×4
	9×1½	1.5 L	23×4
Pie Plate	8×1¼	750 mL	20×3
	9×1¼	1 L	23×3
Baking Dish or Casserole	1 quart	1 L	—
	1½ quart	1.5 L	—
	2 quart	2 L	—